A Let's-Read-and-Find-Out Book™

GERMS MAKE ME SICK!

by Melvin Berger

illustrated by Marylin Hafner

A TRUMPET CLUB SPECIAL EDITION

The *Let's-Read-and-Find-Out Book*™ series was originated by Dr. Franklyn M. Branley, Astronomer Emeritus and former Chairman of the American Museum-Hayden Planetarium, and was formerly co-edited by him and Dr. Roma Gans, Professor Emeritus of Childhood Education, Teachers College, Columbia University. Text and illustrations for each of the more than 100 books in the series are checked for accuracy by an expert in the relevant field. The titles available in paperback are listed below. Look for them at your local bookstore or library.

Air Is All Around You
Ant Cities
A Baby Starts to Grow
The BASIC Book
Bees and Beelines
The Beginning of the Earth
Bits and Bytes
Comets
Corn Is Maize
Danger—Icebergs!
Digging Up Dinosaurs
Dinosaurs Are Different
A Drop of Blood
Ducks Don't Get Wet
Eclipse
Evolution
Fireflies in the Night
Flash, Crash, Rumble, and Roll
Fossils Tell of Long Ago
Get Ready for Robots!

Glaciers
Gravity Is a Mystery
Hear Your Heart
How a Seed Grows
How Many Teeth?
How to Talk to Your Computer
Hurricane Watch
Is There Life in Outer Space?
Journey Into a Black Hole
Look at Your Eyes
Me and My Family Tree
Meet the Computer
The Moon Seems to Change
My Five Senses
My Visit to the Dinosaurs
No Measles, No Mumps for Me
Oxygen Keeps You Alive
The Planets in Our Solar System
Rock Collecting

Rockets and Satellites
The Skeleton Inside You
The Sky Is Full of Stars
Snakes Are Hunters
Snow Is Falling
Straight Hair, Curly Hair
The Sun: Our Nearest Star
Sunshine Makes the Seasons
A Tree Is a Plant
Turtle Talk
Volcanoes
Water for Dinosaurs and You
What Happens to a Hamburger
What I Like About Toads
What Makes Day and Night
What the Moon Is Like
Why Frogs Are Wet
Wild and Woolly Mammoths
Your Skin and Mine

Published by The Trumpet Club
1540 Broadway, New York, New York 10036

ISBN: 0-440-84577-7

This edition published by arrangement with Harper & Row Junior Books, a division of Harper & Row, Publishers, Inc. Printed in the United States of America.   January 1991   UPC   10 9 8 7 6 5 4 3

You wake up one morning. But you don't feel like getting out of bed. Your arms and legs ache. Your head hurts. You have a fever. And your throat is sore.

"I'm sick," you say. "I must have caught a germ."

Everyone knows that germs can make you sick. But not everyone knows how.

Germs are tiny, tiny living beings. They are far too small to see with your eyes alone. In fact, a line of one thousand germs could fit across the top of a pencil!

There are many different kinds of germs. But the two that usually make you sick are bacteria and viruses.

Bacteria are very much like small plants. But they don't look like any plants you know. Under a microscope, some bacteria look like little round balls. Others are as straight as rods. Still others are twisted in spiral shapes.

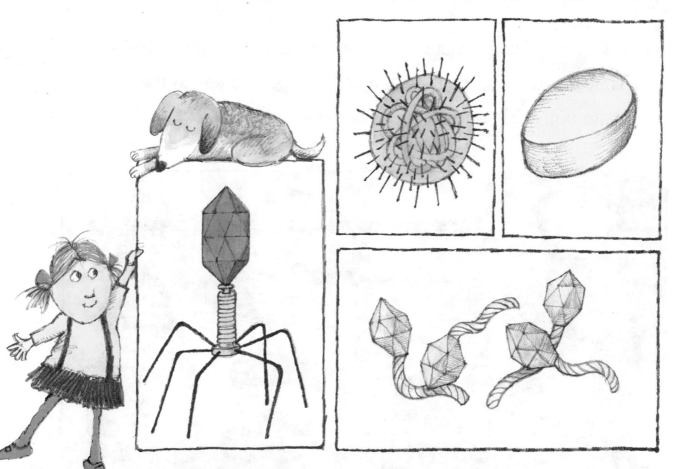

Viruses are far tinier than bacteria. Some look like balls with spikes sticking out on all sides. Others look like loaves of bread or like tadpoles. There are even some that look like metal screws with spider legs.

Germs, such as bacteria and viruses, are found everywhere.
They are in the air you breathe, in the food you eat, in the
water you drink, and on everything you touch.

Although germs are all around, they do not always make you sick. Many germs are not harmful. Also, your body keeps germs out most of the time.

Your skin blocks the germs. As long as there are no cuts or scratches on your skin, germs can't get in.

Your nose helps, too. It is lined with tiny hairs. The hairs catch many of the germs you breathe in. They push them back out.

The inside of your mouth and throat is always wet. Germs often get stuck there. They don't go any farther.

Yet some germs do slip in every once in a while.

Your friend has a cold. He sneezes. Germs fly out. You breathe the air. Some of his germs may get into your lungs.

You take a sip of your cousin's soda. Her germs are on the straw. A few of the germs may get into your stomach.

You're riding a bike. You fall and scrape your knee. Germs from the ground may get under your skin.

But even when harmful bacteria and viruses get into your body, you don't always get sick. That is because your body has ways to fight germs.

The white cells in your blood go after any germs that
sneak in. Usually, these cells kill the germs before they can do
any harm.

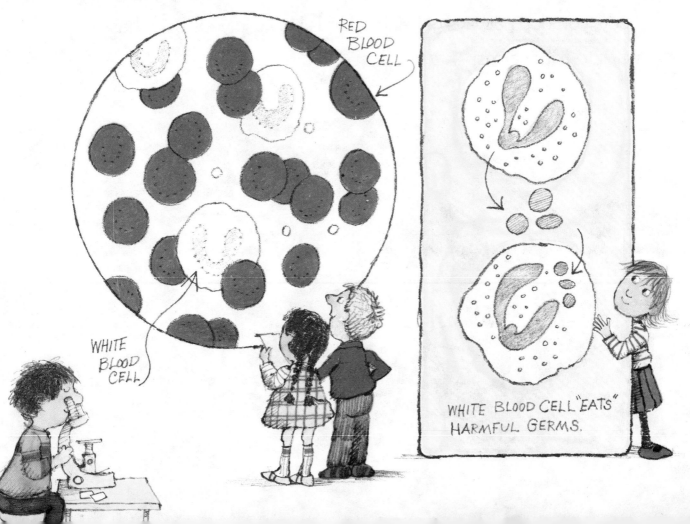

RED
BLOOD
CELL

WHITE
BLOOD
CELL

WHITE BLOOD CELL "EATS"
HARMFUL GERMS.

Your blood also has special chemicals that attack germs. They are called antibodies.

The white blood cells and antibodies don't always get rid of the germs, though. Some germs stay in the body and make you sick.

What if the germs in your body are bacteria? They quickly start to multiply. Each one becomes two new bacteria. Then they become four, and so on. In a few hours there may be *millions* of bacteria in your body.

The bacteria give off waste products. Some of these wastes are poisons. The poisons can damage or kill the cells that make up your body. When enough cells are harmed, you feel sick.

You may have pains and aches, run a fever, or break out in a rash. You may cough or sneeze, or throw up. These signs tell you that cells are being killed in your body.

Some bacteria give off poisons that stay close to the bacteria. Bacteria in your mouth are like that. Their poison only attacks your teeth and causes cavities. It does not go to other places in your body.

Earaches and boils on the skin are also caused by bacteria whose poisons stay in one place.

Other bacteria give off poisons that move around the body. One kind of bacteria lives in the lungs. But it gives off poisons that are carried around in the blood. These bacteria may give you a headache or a sore stomach.

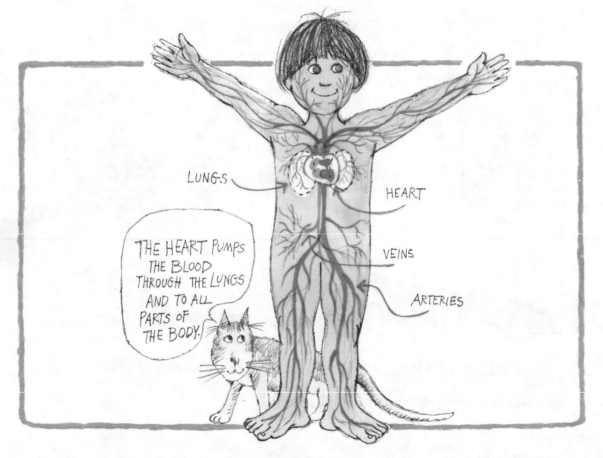

Still other bacteria have poisons in their outer coats. When they touch different cells, their poisons hurt or destroy them. As the cells die, you feel sick.

What if viruses get into your body? Viruses are different from bacteria. They don't give off poisons. Each virus forces its way into a body cell. It disappears inside. For a while, nothing seems to be happening. Then, suddenly, the cell explodes. Hundreds of new viruses tumble out.

Each virus finds another cell and digs its way in. Then these cells pop open, and more viruses pour out. Soon there are *millions* of viruses in your body.

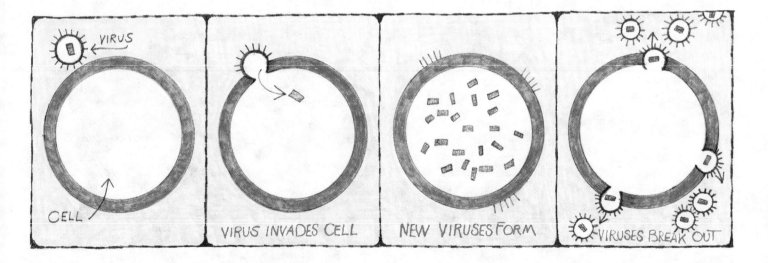

VIRUS INVADES CELL   NEW VIRUSES FORM   VIRUSES BREAK OUT

The viruses spread out. As they do, you feel worse and worse. Viruses bring you colds and the flu, measles, mumps, and chicken pox, and lots of other illnesses.

Though bacteria and viruses can make you sick, you usually begin to feel better after a day or two. Your body has beaten back the germs.

At times, though, you feel *very* sick. Or you stay sick for days. Then you should see a doctor. Doctors try to find out which germs are making you sick.

"What hurts?" they ask. "Let's take a look."

Perhaps they swab your throat with cotton. Then they send the cotton with the germs on it to a lab. Or they may take a few drops of blood from your fingertip or arm. That also goes to a lab to be tested.

Your doctor gets a report from the lab. It tells whether the germs are bacteria or viruses. If bacteria are making you sick, the doctor usually prescribes some drug. The drug will either kill the bacteria or stop them from growing.

Doctors do not yet have drugs to cure diseases caused by viruses. But they can give you shots to prevent some of these diseases.

If you do get sick with a virus, the doctor may give you some medicine anyway. It won't cure you, but it will help you feel better. And it will protect you against bacteria that might make you even sicker.

When germs make you sick, your doctor will tell you to stay in bed. Bed rest makes it easier for your body to fight the germs.

Once you are well, you want to stay that way.

There are lots of ways to keep healthy.

STAY IN LINE, BARBARA.

Germs do make you sick—sometimes. But you can help yourself be as fit as a fiddle all the rest of the time!